OpenCourt Reading

e:
nd
ills

tion

A Division of The McGraw-Hill Companies

Columbus, Ohio

www.sra4kids.com

SRA/McGraw-Hill

A Division of The McGraw·Hill Companies

Copyright © 2002 by SRA/McGraw-Hill.

Send all inquiries to:
SRA/McGraw-Hill
8787 Orion Place
Columbus, OH 43240-4027

Printed in the United States of America.

ISBN 0-07-572051-5

2 3 4 5 6 7 8 9 QPD 07 06 05 04 03 02

Table of Contents

Name _____ Date _____

▶Capital Letters

MECHANICS

Directions: The new swimming team list has just been posted. Rewrite the list of names correctly.

<u>Sea Ponies</u>

Capital Letters • Challenge: Comprehension and Language Arts Skills

▶ Writing Words

Directions: Draw pictures of four different animals. Write the word that names each animal.

1. ___Answers will vary.___

2. ___Answers will vary.___

3. ___Answers will vary.___

4. ___Answers will vary.___

WRITER'S CRAFT

UNIT I Let's Read! • **Lesson 6** *There Was Once a Fish*

▶Capital Letters: Cities and States

MECHANICS

1. _____K_____ kansas

2. _____W_____ washington

3. _____M_____ miami

4. _____S_____ sacramento

5. _____N_____ newark

6. _____C_____ colorado

Name _____ Date _____

▶Order Words

Directions: Draw four pictures that tell what you do when you come to school in the morning. Draw them so that they are in order. Label them first, next, then, and last.

1. _____ **first** _____

2. _____ **next** _____

3. _____ **then** _____

4. _____ **last** _____

WRITER'S CRAFT

▶ Sentences

1. john sits on the dock

_____

John sits on the dock.

2. amber rings the bells

_____

Amber rings the bells.

3. the bus waits for Jill

_____

The bus waits for Jill.

Sentences • Challenge: Comprehension
and Language Arts Skills

▶ Sentences

The boy	She	spins	mops

1. _____
   She plays.

2. The top _____
   spins .

3. _____
   The boy sits.

4. Dad _____
   mops .

WRITER'S CRAFT

UNIT 1 Let's Read! • **Lesson 14** *Mrs. Goose's Baby*

▶Comparing and Contrasting

Directions: In the rows that begin with A, circle the two pictures that are alike. In the rows that begin with D, circle the one picture that is different.

COMPREHENSION

A

A

D

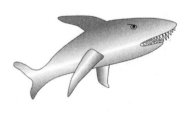

D

Comparing and Contrasting • Challenge: Comprehension and Language Arts Skills

▶ Adjectives

Directions: Use the adjectives **hot** or **cold** to complete each sentence. Then write the name of one more thing that these adjectives can describe.

hot	cold

1. Grant sits in the _____ hot _____ sun.

2. Grant is drinking _____ cold _____ juice.

3. The _____ cold _____ snow makes me shiver.

4. A cup of _____ hot _____ cocoa will taste good.

5. hot _____ Accept reasonable answers. _____

6. cold _____ Accept reasonable answers. _____

GRAMMAR AND USAGE

WRITER'S CRAFT

▶ Using Adjectives

Answers will vary and may include colors,
textures, patterns, and sizes.

1. _____   2. _____

Students should write adjectives that
describe the clothing in the picture.

3. _____   4. _____

Using Adjectives • Challenge: Comprehension
and Language Arts Skills

UNIT 2 Animals • **Lesson 6** *Munch Crunch: The Foods Animals Eat*

▶Types of Sentences

Directions: Draw a picture of yourself. Complete each sentence.

GRAMMAR AND USAGE

1. _____

I have ____ **Accept appropriate telling sentences.** ____ .

2. _____

Do you ____ **Accept appropriate asking sentences.** ____ ?

3. _____

I love **Accept appropriate sentences that show strong feeling.** ____ !

▶Main Idea and Details

COMPREHENSION

1. Main Idea: A birthday party
Details:

2. Main Idea: Going on a picnic
Details:

Main Idea and Details • Challenge: Comprehension
and Language Arts Skills

▶ Writing Sentences

Directions: Write the correct end mark for each sentence. Then write one of the telling sentences, one of the strong feeling sentences, and the asking sentence.

Our raft is fast __.__ Look out __!__ We
hit a bump __.__ Our raft is stuck **. or !**
What can we do __?__ We can lift the
raft __.__ Then on we can go __.__

WRITER'S CRAFT

1. telling

_____

- -
Accept any of the telling sentences.
_____

2. strong feeling

_____

- -
Look out! or Our raft is stuck!
_____

3. asking

_____

- -
What can we do?
_____

UNIT 2 Animals • **Lesson II** *Spiders*

▶**Review**

Directions: Use the adjectives to complete each sentence. Write the correct end marks after each sentence. Then, draw a picture to match your descriptions.

GRAMMAR AND USAGE

green	furry	brown	big

Ruth has a _____ dog, a _____ cat,

a _____ rabbit, and a _____

**Accept an appropriate
adjective for each line.**

fish ___·___

There are pets everywhere __!__ Do you

have any pets __?__

picture should match descriptions

Review • Challenge: Comprehension
and Language Arts Skills

▶ Writing Descriptions

Directions: Look at the pictures. Write the words that describe it on the line.

| warm fuzzy |
| red crunchy |
| big yellow |
| fast brown |

1. big yellow

2. warm fuzzy

3. red crunchy

4. fast brown

UNIT 2 Animals • **Lesson 14** *The Hermit Crab*

▶Drawing Conclusions

COMPREHENSION

1. The children are planting a garden.   (Yes)   No

2. There are three children.   (Yes)   No

3. It is cold outside.   Yes   (No)

4. The children are wearing coats.   Yes   (No)

5. The children are staying clean.   Yes   (No)

UNIT 3 Things That Go • **Lesson 1** *Unit Introduction*

▶ Possessive Nouns

Ben  hat

1.

_____

- -

Ben's hat

Pam  gift

2.

_____

- -

Pam's gift

3.

_____

- -

possessive of student's name and item they have drawn

GRAMMAR AND USAGE

Challenge: Comprehension • *Possessive Nouns*
and Language Arts Skills

▶Staying on Topic

WRITER'S CRAFT

Things With Wheels

trucks

skates

_____

- - - - - - - - - - - - - -

_____

- - - - - - - - - - - - - -

_____

Answers will vary and may include cars, bikes, motorcycles or other vehicles with wheels.

Things With Wings

planes

bees

_____

- - - - - - - - - - - - - -

_____

- - - - - - - - - - - - - -

_____

Answers will vary and may include birds, jets, insects, and so on.

Staying on Topic • Challenge: Comprehension and Language Arts Skills

UNIT 3 Things That Go • **Lesson 6** *Song of the Train*

▶Singular and Plural Nouns

| boy | tree | bike | girl | flag | wheel |

Directions: Read the words in the box and look at the picture. Add **s** to words that show more than one and write them on the lines.

trees, bikes, wheels (any order)

_____

_____

_____

Challenge: Comprehension • *Singular and Plural Nouns* and Language Arts Skills

UNIT 3 Things That Go • **Lesson 8** *On the Go*

▶ Sensory Details

WRITER'S CRAFT

Directions: Draw a picture of your favorite food. Write words that tell how it looks, smells, tastes, feels, and sounds when you eat it.

Students should write sentences that use sensory words to

tell about the food. Answers may include sweet, salty, sour,

crunchy, soft, warm, cold, yummy, munch, and so on.

▶Comparing and Contrasting

Directions: Circle the thing in each row that is different. Then, below, circle the word or words that tell how the things in each row are alike.

COMPREHENSION

1.  (circled)

2.    (circled)

3.    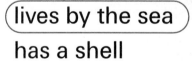 (circled)

4.  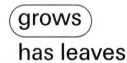   (lives by the sea)
has a shell

5.      (grows)
has leaves

6.   (pie)   (foods)
desserts

Name _____ Date _____

GRAMMAR AND USAGE

Directions: Look at the pictures and read the words. Add an 's to the words that tell who owns something. Add s to the nouns that show more than one. Write the possessive phrase on the line.

▶ Review

1. Henry  cat

_____

- -

Henry's cats

2. Lucy  cot

_____

- -

Lucy's cot

3. cat  bowl

_____

- -

cat's bowl

4. Dad  book

_____

- -

Dad's books

_____

Review • Challenge: Comprehension
and Language Arts Skills

▶Order Words

next	last	first	then

Possible answers:

_____
- - - - - - - - - - - - - -
Then or Next

1. _____ I turn on the light.

_____
- - - - - - - - - - - - - -
First

2. _____ I wake up in the morning.

_____
- - - - - - - - - - - - - -
Last

3. _____ I eat breakfast.

_____
- - - - - - - - - - - - - -
Next or Then

4. _____ I let the cat out.

WRITER'S CRAFT

▶Capitalization

MECHANICS

My Birthday

Directions: Look at your classroom calendar. Find your birthday. Write the day and month. Draw a picture of what you did or plan to do on your birthday.

Accept all reasonable pictures.

Day of the Week _____ Answers will vary. _____

Month of the Year _____ Answers will vary. _____

Capital Letters • Challenge: Comprehension and Language Arts Skills

▶ Classifying and Categorizing

Directions: Look at the first picture in each row. Then, circle a picture in each row that belongs with the first picture.

1.

2.

3.

4.

5.

COMPREHENSION

▶ Who, What, Where and When

WRITER'S CRAFT

What? a party for Rosa
When? Sunday, April 23
       2:00pm
Where? 74 Bennett Street

1. Who? Rosa

2. What? a party

3. When? Sunday, April 23, 2:00

4. Where? 74 Bennett St.

Name _____ Date _____

▶ End Punctuation

Directions: Read each sentence and write the correct end mark. Then, write a sentence that tells what Tom can do so that the dog does not get his bag again.

MECHANICS

1. **What is the dog doing** _____ **?** _____

2. **The dog has Tom's bag** _____ **.**

3. **Bad dog** _____ **!** _____

Sentences may vary; may use a period or exclamation point.

_____

_____

WRITER'S CRAFT

▶ Structure of a Personal Letter

Your friend,

James

Thank you for coming to visit our class. I learned a lot about your job. I want to be a reporter someday too.

Dear Mrs. Hill,

> **Students should have all parts of a letter correctly placed: greeting, message, and closing.**

Name _____ Date _____

▶ Review

Directions: Read the schedule for story hour. Look for mistakes in capitalization. Write the correct day or month. Write the correct end mark for each sentence.

Story hour in may is all about animals!

mondays- stories about pets

fridays- stories about farm animals

1. You can hear stories about animals in

_____

_ _ _ _ _ _ _ _ _ _ _ _ _

_____ **May** _____ __.__

2. When can you hear stories about pets __?__

_____

_ _ _ _ _ _ _ _ _ _ _ _ _

3. Stories about pets are on _____ **Mondays** _____ __.__

4. When can you hear stories about farm animals __?__

5. Stories about farm animals are on

_____

_ _ _ _ _ _ _ _ _ _ _ _ _

___ **Fridays** _____ __.__

▶ # Audience and Purpose

WRITER'S CRAFT

Purpose

1. invitation _____

Answers may vary. The purpose should be appropriate for the type of writing.

2. list _____

3. story _____

Audience

4. letter _____

Answers may vary. The audience should be appropriate for the type of writing.

5. poster _____

6. learning log _____

Audience and Purpose • Challenge: Comprehension and Language Arts Skills

▶ Longer Sentences

Directions: Use the words to write sentences that tell how, when, or where.

to work	every day	safely

My mom drives a van.

_____

1. How? My mom drives a van safely.

_____

2. When? My mom drives a van every day.

_____

3. Where? My mom drives a van to work.

in music class	very well

We sing songs.

_____

4. How? We sing songs very well.

_____

5. Where? We sing songs in music class.

WRITER'S CRAFT

▶ Adjectives

Directions: Read each word and look at the picture. Write two adjectives from the box that describe each picture.

hot	soft	smooth	furry
	spicy	shiny	

_____

hot

_____

spicy

_____

soft

_____

furry

_____

smooth

_____

shiny

Adjectives • Challenge: Comprehension
and Language Arts Skills

GRAMMAR AND USAGE

UNIT 5 **Weather • Lesson 2** *When a Storm Comes Up*

▶ Main Idea and Details

1. Main idea: Building a House
Details:

2. Main idea: Planting a Garden
Details:

COMPREHENSION

▶Order Words

WRITER'S CRAFT

| then | first | next | last |

We want to give our dog Benny a bath.
_____

First
_____, we fill the tub with water.
_____

Then
_____, we get the soap.
_____

next
The _____ thing we do is find Benny.
_____

Last
_____, we put Benny in the tub.

Order Words • Challenge: Comprehension
and Language Arts Skills

▶Verbs

GRAMMAR AND USAGE

Directions: Write the best action word to complete each sentence on the line. Then write your own sentence about someone who helps you. Circle the action word in your sentence.

cuts	show	help	looks	cleans

_____

1. People _____ **help** _____ us every day.

2. Teachers _____ **show** _____ me how to do new things.

3. The barber _____ **cuts** _____ my hair.

4. The dentist _____ **cleans** _____ my teeth.

5. The doctor _____ **looks** _____ in my ears.

_____

Sentences will vary; the verb should be circled.

▶ Review

GRAMMAR AND USAGE

Directions: Write an adjective that describes each picture. Then, write a sentence that tells about an action each animal might do. Circle the action word in your sentence. The first one is done for you.

The silly monkey (swings) on the branch.   silly

Accept an appropriate adjective.

Sentences will vary; the verb should be circled.

Accept an appropriate adjective.

Sentences will vary; the verb should be circled.

Accept an appropriate adjective.

Sentences will vary; the verb should be circled.

▶ Commas in a Series

Directions: Write a sentence that tells what Mom bought at the grocery store. Then, write a grocery list of your own and write a sentence telling what you will buy.

Mom's Grocery List

milk

jelly

bananas

ham

Mom bought milk, bananas, jelly, and ham.

Accept any reasonable wording.

My Grocery List

Grocery items will vary.

Sentence should list grocery items

using commas in a series.

MECHANICS

▶Classifying and Categorizing

COMPREHENSION

things for drawing things for winter	things in a kitchen things in the water

1.

_____

things in a kitchen

_____

2.

_____

things for winter

Classifying and Categorizing • Challenge: Comprehension and Language Arts Skills

▶ A Paragraph That Explains

Directions: Read the sentences. Write them in the correct order to make a paragraph that explains. Write a sentence at the beginning to tell about the topic you are writing.

Last, I put them in the suitcase.

First, I gather all of the clothes I want to pack.

Then, I fold them neatly.

WRITER'S CRAFT

Topic sentences will vary. Examples: I am going to
pack for a trip. This is how I pack my bag, etc.
The sentences should be written: First, I gather all of the
clothes I want to pack. Then, I fold them neatly.
Last, I put them in the suitcase.

▶ Cities and States

Directions: Read the story. Circle each letter that should be a capital. Then, write the name of the city and state where you were born.

MECHANICS

My family has moved around a lot. Each child in my family was born in a different state. My brother Josh was born in dallas, texas. My sister Kate was born in portland, oregon. Then came my sister Anne. She was born in witchita, kansas. I was born next in lexington, kentucky. At last came my brother Seth. He was born in tampa, florida.

_____

I was born in _____ Names of city and state will vary. _____ .

Cities and States • Challenge: Comprehension and Language Arts Skills

▶ Place and Location Words

above	below	beside	in	on
over	under	behind		

Answers will vary. Students should use an appropriate position word to describe the location of each item.

1. clock

_____

2. door

_____

3. coats

_____

4. chalkboard

_____

5. shelves

_____

WRITER'S CRAFT

Name _____ Date _____

▶ Making Inferences

Answers
will vary.
Possible answers:

1. _____ Grandma stubbed her toe on the farm. _____

2. _____ Joe stopped working to help Grandma. _____

Making Inferences • **Challenge: Comprehension
and Language Arts Skills**

▶Review

I have visited

_____ _____

- -

Names of city and state will vary.

_____ , _____ .

I saw

_____

- -

Check for correct usage of commas in a series.

_____ .

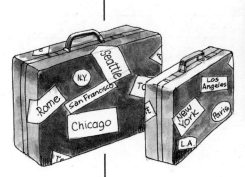

MECHANICS

▶ Form of a Paragraph

Directions: Circle the sentences that go together. Then write all of the sentences in a paragraph.

WRITER'S CRAFT

(Our class took a trip to see a play.)

(We rode on a bus to the theater.)

I can play soccer.

(We all watched the play.)

I like to eat grapes.

(It was a fun day.)

_____

- -

_____

Our class took a trip to see a play. We rode on a bus to

the theater. We all watched the play. It was a fun day.

_____

- -

_____

- -

_____

- -

_____

Form of a Paragraph • **Challenge: Comprehension and Language Arts Skills**

▶Past Tense Verbs

Draw a picture of two things that you have done today. Write a sentence about each picture. Circle the verbs that tell that it already happened.

Picture and sentence should be about a past event;
past tense verb should be circled.

Picture and sentence should be about a past event;
past tense verb should be circled.

▶Concept Words

▶A game is "a way of amusing oneself." Write a list of words that describe the concept of a game.

_____
Answers will vary; possible answers:
- -
rules, players, compete, score.
_____

_____

_____

_____

▶Write a sentence using one of the words on your list to tell about a game that you have played.

_____

Sentences will vary.
_____

_____

_____

_____

▶Sound Spelling Review

▶Fill in the blanks with the correct long-
or short-vowel spelling.

ee	o	i	a

Mike ___a___nd I went to the fair at thr___ee___

o'clock. We each played s___i___x games and got a

fr___ee___ balloon. I wr___o___te about our day in my

journal. I can't wait to g___o___ to the fair again.

▶Write a rhyming word with the same spelling pattern.

Answers
will vary.

1. and _____ **2.** go _____

SPELLING

▶ Exact Words

Choose the word that describes the picture.
Then use the word in a sentence.

leaped	icy	slithered	sticky

Sentences will vary.

_____

1. _____

Sentence should include the word *sticky*.

_____

2. _____

Sentence should include the word *slithered*.

_____

3. _____

Sentence should include the word *leaped*.

_____

4. _____

Sentence should include the word *icy*.

_____

Exact Words • Challenge: Comprehension
and Language Arts Skills

▶Cause and Effect

Read the sentence that tells what happened.

Then, write a sentence that explains why.

Accept any reasonable answers.

1. The dog is wet and muddy.

_____

- -

The dog was out in the rain.

_____

2. The grass is tall.

_____

- -

The grass has not been cut.

_____

3. The leaves are falling off the tree.

_____

- -

It is fall.

_____

4. Mom is mad at Peppy the dog.

_____

- -

Peppy broke the vase.

_____

COMPREHENSION

▶ Antonyms

VOCABULARY

▶ **Write the correct antonym on the line.**

1. When I'm not **happy**, I'm ____ sad ____.

2. I was **clean**, but now I'm ____ dirty ____.

3. The grass is **short** and the tree is ____ tall ____.

4. You can't **stay**; you must ____ go ____.

▶ **Write two more pairs of antonyms.**

_____   _____

        Antonyms will vary.

_____   _____

_____   _____

▶Sound Spelling Review

▶ Read the words. Circle the words that have the /ū/ sound.

(cue)	city	water
cone	(cute)	(use)
(few)	(pure)	kitten
swim	plant	(pew)

▶ Write a sentence using one or two of the /ū/ words above.

_____

- -

Sentences will vary.

_____

_____

- -

_____

SPELLING

▶ Pronouns

Write the pronoun that takes the place of the underlined word or words.

them	it	she	they

1. <u>Josh, Pete, and Shane</u> went to the game.

_____

They _____ went to the game.

I went with _____ them _____.

2. <u>Jan</u> plays the flute.

_____

She _____ plays the flute.

3. <u>The cat</u> takes a long nap.

_____

It _____ takes a long nap.

▶Staying on Topic

Read the sentence. Write sentences that stay on topic.

It was a cold, snowy day.

Students should write sentences in
the paragraph that stay on topic.

Students may write about snow, cold,
books, staying indoors, and so on.

WRITER'S CRAFT

COMPREHENSION

▶Drawing Conclusions

Read the story. Circle the best answers.

Jill's Birthday

Jill's birthday is on Saturday. She is going to have a birthday party. Many friends are going to come.

The week passes slowly. Jill gets more and more excited. On Friday morning Jill wakes up with a fever. Jill and her mom don't want Jill's friends to get sick too. They postpone the party until the next Saturday. Jill is sad.

Next Saturday Jill is well. She and her friends have lots of fun at Jill's birthday party.

1. Why was Jill excited during the week?
   a. for her birthday **b.** for the circus **c.** for the park

2. Why did Jill and her mom postpone the party?
   a. So that no one else would get sick.
   b. So that they could celebrate alone.
   c. So that Jill could have two birthday parties.

UNIT 7 Keep Trying • **Lesson 4** *The Garden*

▶ Parts of a Group

▶ **Draw a picture of your school.**

▶ **Write words that name things in your school.**

answers will vary; possible answers: teachers,

students, desks, chairs, books, pencils

SPELLING

► Sound Spelling Review

► Sometimes words with the same spelling patterns have different sounds. Say each word. Circle the words that have the same vowel sound as the spelling word.

1. n<u>ow</u>   (h<u>ow</u>)   (c<u>ow</u>)   sl<u>ow</u>

2. gr<u>ee</u>n   b<u>ee</u>n   (qu<u>ee</u>n)   (s<u>ee</u>n)

► Write two more words with the same vowel sound and spelling pattern as each of the words below.

_____   _____

3. fr<u>og</u>   Answers will vary.   _____

_____   _____

4. t<u>oa</u>d   _____   _____

_____   _____

5. s<u>un</u>   _____   _____

_____   _____

6. w<u>ill</u>   _____   _____

Sound Spelling Review • Challenge: Comprehension and Language Arts Skills

▶Possessive Pronouns

Look at the picture. Read the sentence. Write the possessive pronoun and what is owned.

your	her	his	its

1. Carlos has a pet bird. _____
his pet bird

2. A zebra has stripes. _____
its stripes

3. Asha has a ball. _____
her ball

4. You have a coach. _____
your coach

GRAMMAR AND USAGE

▶Sentences

Draw a picture of your favorite kind of weather.
Write two sentences to tell about it.

WRITER'S CRAFT

1. _____ Students should write complete sentences.
_____

_____ The sentences should have a naming part and
_____

2. _____ action part, begin with a capital letter, and end
_____

_____ with an end mark.

Sentences • Challenge: Comprehension
and Language Arts Skills

▶Main Idea and Details

Place an X next to the details that support each main idea.

1. Main Idea: Pets
Details:

__X__ cat

_____ pencil

_____ flower

__X__ dog

__X__ fish

2. Main Idea: Parts of the Body
Details:

__X__ arm

__X__ leg

_____ popcorn

__X__ ear

_____ cup

3. Main Idea: In a Park
Details:

__X__ benches

__X__ grass

_____ desk

_____ ladder

__X__ trees

4. Main Idea: In a Kitchen
Details:

__X__ dishes

_____ sofa

__X__ stove

_____ bed

__X__ sink

COMPREHENSION

▶ Parts of a Group

VOCABULARY

▶ Draw a picture of a playground that has:

| swings | trees | flowers | grass | slide |

[drawing box]

▶ Write the words that name things that grow.

_____ _____ _____

- -

tree, flowers, grass; any order

▶ Write the words that name things that
are things to play on.

_____ _____

- -

swings, slide; any order

▶Adjectives that Compare

GRAMMAR AND USAGE

Read the words in the box. Add *-er* or *-est* to the words to complete each sentence.

long	tall	fast	old

Our class saw many animals at the zoo. Zora

_____

is the _____ oldest _____ ape in the zoo.

_____

The giraffe has a _____ longer _____

neck than the zebra. The cheetah runs

_____

_____ faster _____ than the lion. Two

monkeys played in the _____ tallest _____ tree

in the zoo. Our class loved the trip to the zoo.

▶Sound Spelling Review

Read the story. Circle the words with the /s/ sound spelled *ce* or *ci_*. Draw a line under the words with the /ow/ sound spelled *ow* or *ou_*.

Last week, my family went <u>down</u> to the (city) to see the (circus.) We saw <u>clowns</u> with painted (faces) and <u>flowers</u> in their hats. The short <u>clown</u> <u>frowned</u> when his hat fell on the <u>ground</u>. I <u>found</u> fifty (cents,) so I (raced) to the snack bar to get some popcorn. I made it back in time to see the <u>clowns</u> take a <u>bow</u>. "What a fun (place!)" I <u>shouted</u>.

▶Longer Sentences

Look at the picture. Write sentences that tell how, when, and where the children get ready for school.

1. _____
   Sentences will vary. Students should use
   _____

   _____
   words that tell how, when, and where in their
   _____

2. _____
   sentences. Examples: quickly, slowly, at home,
   _____

   _____
   in the morning, everyday, and so on.
   _____

WRITER'S CRAFT

▶Sequence

▶ **Put the sentences in order. Use 1–5.**

COMPREHENSION

__3__ Miss Jane and the children push the raft into the river.

__5__ Miss Jane and the children finish their raft ride.

__1__ Miss Jane drives the children to the river.

__4__ Miss Jane starts rowing the raft into the river while the children hold on tightly.

__2__ Miss Jane and the children review the safety rules and collect their helmets and life jackets.

▶Antonyms

▶Write the antonym that makes sense in each sentence.

sour   sweet

Too many _____sweet_____ foods can hurt your teeth.

The grapes were too _____sour_____ .

shy   bold

The _____shy_____ kitten was hiding.

The _____bold_____ cat jumped at the dog.

▶**Write two more pairs of antonyms.**

Antonyms will vary; possible answers:

tall, short; day, night; stop, go; and so on.

_____   _____

VOCABULARY

▶Review

Write the word that completes each sentence.

her	faster	played	they

1. Yesterday the children ___played___ at the park.

2. ___They___ had fun.

3. Sue brought ___her___ ball.

4. Laura ran ___faster___ than Kevin.

Review • Challenge: Comprehension
and Language Arts Skills

UNIT 7 Keep Trying • **Lesson 9** *Unit Wrap-Up*

▶Sound Spelling Review

▶ Circle the words with the /oo/ sound. Draw
a line under the words with the /o͞o/ sound.

<u>soon</u>   (book)   <u>goose</u>   (cook)

(foot)   <u>balloon</u>   (look)   <u>too</u>

▶ Write a sentence using a word with the /oo/ sound.

_____

- -
Sentences will vary.
_____

▶ Write a sentence using a word with the /o͞o/ sound.

_____

- -
Sentences will vary.
_____

▶ Say each word. Draw a line from each spelling word
to the word that has the same vowel sound.

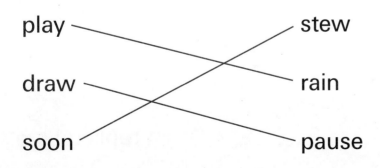

SPELLING

▶Dialogue

Look at the picture of Mom, Ben, and Lara. Write words that each person says. Use quotation marks.

Sentences will vary. Check to see that students have placed quotation marks correctly.

- -

1. _____ , said Lara.

_____

- -

2. _____ , asked Ben.

_____

- -

3. Mom said, _____ .

_____

- -

4. _____ , replied Lara.

WRITER'S CRAFT

▶Kinds of Sentences

▶**Write a sentence that tells something about the animals.**

_____

Answers will vary; sentence should end with a period.

_____

▶**Write a sentence that asks something about the animals.**

_____

Answers will vary; sentence should end with a
question mark.

_____

▶**Write a sentence about the animals that shows strong feeling.**

_____

Answers will vary; sentence should end with an
exclamation point.

_____

▶Sequence

▶Put the sentences in order.
Use 1, 2, 3, 4, 5.

__3__ We spoon the mixture into muffin tins.

__1__ We gather flour, oil, honey, bananas, and spices.

__4__ The muffins bake for 30 minutes.

__2__ We mash the bananas and then add everything else.

__5__ Our muffins taste good with glasses of milk.

__5__ She touches home plate and the crowd cheers.

__2__ She waits for the perfect pitch.

__3__ She swings and sends the ball flying.

__1__ A batter steps up to the plate.

__4__ The batter runs to all the bases.

Sequence • Challenge: Comprehension
and Language Arts Skills

UNIT 8 Games • **Lesson 2** *A Game Called Piggle*

▶Synonyms

▶ **Read each sentence. Write a synonym**
for each underlined word.
Synonyms may vary.

1. The knife is <u>pointy</u>.

_____
- - - - - - - - - - - - -
sharp
_____

2. Mom likes to <u>chat</u> on the phone.

- - - - - - - - - - - - -
talk
_____

3. It is <u>chilly</u> outside today.

- - - - - - - - - - - - -
cold
_____

4. I packed my lunch in a <u>sack</u>.

- - - - - - - - - - - - -
bag
_____

5. The red <u>carpet</u> is soft.

- - - - - - - - - - - - -
rug
_____

6. We had steak for <u>supper</u>.

- - - - - - - - - - - - -
dinner
_____

VOCABULARY

Challenge: Comprehension • *Synonyms*
and Language Arts Skills

UNIT 8 Games • **Lesson 2** *A Game Called Piggle*

WRITER'S CRAFT

▶Sensory Words

▶Draw a picture of a place you like to go to.
Write words that tell how things look,
taste, feel, smell, and sound at this place.

Answers will vary. Check to see that students have used

sensory details to describe the places that they drew.

Sensory Words • Challenge: Comprehension
and Language Arts Skills

▶Comparing and Contrasting

▶Circle the pictures that are alike. Write a sentence telling how they are alike.

Answers will vary. Possible answer:

Both are hats.

▶Circle the picture that is different. Write a sentence telling how it is different.

Answers will vary. Possible answer:

People live in this house.

COMPREHENSION

▶ Sound Spelling Review

▶**Read each sentence. Circle the misspelled word.**
Write the word correctly in a sentence of your own.

SPELLING

1. I want to go to the park with my (famly).

_____

- -

sentence using "family"

_____

2. I'd rather (swinn) at the park.

_____

- -

sentence using "swing"

_____

3. Do you (knoe) how to get to the park?

_____

- -

sentence using "know"

_____

4. Miss Pond got us a bunch of (purpl) grapes.

_____

- -

sentence using "purple"

_____

▶Sentence Parts

▶Write an action part for each naming part.

1. The hungry dog _____ Answers will vary. _____.

2. Sally and Max _____ Answers will vary. _____.

3. The police car _____ Answers will vary. _____.

▶Write a naming part for each action part.

4. _____ Answers will vary. _____ went to the store.

5. _____ Answers will vary. _____ ate all the lettuce in our garden.

6. _____ Answers will vary. _____ splashed in the water.

GRAMMAR AND USAGE

▶Antonyms

VOCABULARY

▶Read each sentence. Rewrite the sentence using an antonym of the underlined word. Draw a line under the antonym. The first one is done for you.

1. Ian can <u>push</u> the cart.

_____

Ian can <u>pull</u> the cart.

Sentences may vary; possible answers are given.

2. My dad is <u>tall</u>.

_____

My dad is <u>short</u>.

3. I was <u>wrong</u>.

_____

I was <u>right</u>.

4. The truck beeps when it goes <u>backward</u>.

_____

The truck beeps when it goes <u>forward</u>.

Antonyms • Challenge: Comprehension and Language Arts Skills

▶ Sound Spelling Review

▶ Add *ph* or *wr_* to complete each word.

_____   _____

_____ ph _____ rase   _____ wr _____ inkle

_____ wr _____ ite   _____ ph _____ one

gra _____ ph _____   _____ wr _____ ench

▶ Write a sentence using a word with the
/f/ sound spelled *ph*.

_____

Sentences will vary.

▶ Write a sentence using a word with the
/r/ sound spelled *wr_*.

_____

Sentences will vary.

SPELLING

▶ Homophones

▶ **Read each sentence. Write the correct homophone on the line.**

where	right	piece
wear	write	peace

I. I am going to _____ wear _____ a hat today.

2. Do they know _____ where _____ to go?

3. I like to _____ write _____ stories.

4. I have the _____ right _____ answer.

5. May I have a _____ piece _____ of pie?

6. Mom wants some _____ peace _____ and quiet.

VOCABULARY

▶Sound Spelling Review

▶Circle the word that rhymes with each spelling word. Then write another word that rhymes with the spelling word on the line.

SPELLING

1. ran   (plan)   plane

_____
Rhyming words will vary.
_____

2. sit   bite   (bit)

_____
Rhyming words will vary.
_____

3. win   (twin)   twine

_____
Rhyming words will vary.
_____

4. not   (tot)   tote

_____
Rhyming words will vary.
_____

5. can   mane   (man)

_____
Rhyming words will vary.
_____

6. let   (set)   seat

_____
Rhyming words will vary.
_____

Challenge: Comprehension • *Sound Spelling Review* and Language Arts Skills

GRAMMAR USAGE

►Contractions

► Write the words that make each contraction. Then write a sentence using one of the contractions.

1. isn't   is not

2. didn't   did not

3. shouldn't   should not

4. won't   will not

5. can't   can not

6. don't   do not

Sentences will vary.

Contractions • Challenge: Comprehension and Language Arts Skills

UNIT 8 Games • **Lesson 6** *The Great Ball Game*

▶Repeating Sounds

▶Draw a picture of an animal. Write words
that start with the same sound to describe it.

WRITER'S CRAFT

Answers will vary based on the animal used. Check to see

that students have written words with repeating sounds.

UNIT 8 Games • **Lesson 7** *The Big Team Relay Race*

▶ Cause and Effect

▶**Tell why each picture happened. Write a sentence.**

Accept any reasonable wording.

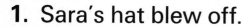

1. Sara's hat blew off.

_____

- - - - - - - - - - - - - - - - - - -

It is a windy day.

_____

2. The cat ran up the tree.

_____

- - - - - - - - - - - - - - - - - - -

The dog chased the cat.

_____

3. Tom cut his leg.

_____

- - - - - - - - - - - - - - - - - - -

Tom fell down.

_____

4. The car has a flat tire.

_____

- - - - - - - - - - - - - - - - - - -

The car ran over a nail.

_____

Cause and Effect • Challenge: Comprehension and Language Arts Skills

COMPREHENSION

▶Synonyms and Antonyms

▶Write a pair of synonyms. Write a sentence using each synonym.

_____   _____

Synonyms will vary; check for meaning.

_____   _____

1. _____ Sentences will vary; check for meaning.

_____

2. _____ Sentences will vary; check for meaning.

_____

▶Write a pair of antonyms. Write a sentence using each antonym.

_____   _____

Antonyms will vary; check for meaning.

_____   _____

1. _____ Sentences will vary; check for meaning.

_____

2. _____ Sentences will vary; check for meaning.

_____

VOCABULARY

UNIT 8 Games • **Lesson 7** *The Big Team Relay Race*

GRAMMAR AND USAGE

▶Review

▶Read each sentence. Write the correct end mark.

1. Why did you turn off the light ____ **?** ____

2. I love to write ____ **.** ____

▶Complete the sentence with a naming part.

3. ____ sentences will vary ____ swam to the shore.

▶Write the correct contraction.

4. I will ____ **I'll** ____

5. we are ____ **we're** ____

Review • Challenge: Comprehension
and Language Arts Skills

▶A Paragraph that Describes

▶Draw a picture of your favorite toy.
  Write a paragraph to describe it.

My favorite toy is

Check to see that the first sentence identifies the toy, the
other sentences describe the toy, and the last sentence
refers back to the first sentence.

SPELLING

▶Sound Spelling Review

▶**Change the underlined letter or letters to create new words.**

1. l̲ine

_____ Answers will vary; possible answers _____
include: fine, mine, vine, and so on.
_____ _____

_____ Answers will vary; possible answers _____
include: law, straw, and so on.

2. d̲raw

▶**Circle the words that have the /m/ sound spelled *mb*. Draw a line under the words that have the /ē/ sound spelled *ea*.**

(lamb)   drum   e̲a̲c̲h̲   (plumber)

e̲a̲t̲   (thumb)   greet   t̲e̲a̲m̲

▶**Write a sentence using one of the circled words and write another sentence using an underlined word.**

_____

_ _

Sentences will vary.

_____

_ _

Sentences will vary.

_____

Name _____ Date _____

▶ Review

▶Write words that name people, places, and things.
Each list has been started for you.

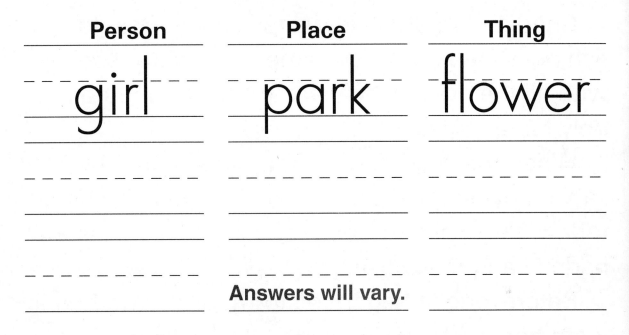

Person	Place	Thing
girl	park	flower

Answers will vary.

▶Write a sentence using one of the nouns on your
list. For example: The *girl* is happy.

Sentences will vary.

▶Rewrite your sentence using a pronoun in place of
the noun. For example: *She* is happy.

Sentence should use a pronoun.

GRAMMAR AND USAGE

▶ Drawing Conclusions

▶**Read the story. Circle the best answers.**

Chad and Kristin Go Fishing

Chad and Kristin had waited all week to go fishing. When Saturday came, they were ready with all their gear. The walk to the stream took only ten minutes.

When the children reached the stream, they saw many people fishing. "The fish must be biting today," they said. An hour later, Chad and Kristin hadn't caught any fish.

Before long, it began to storm. Chad and Kristin went home. They were sad, but they knew they could fish again another day.

1. How do Chad and Kristin feel when Saturday comes?

   a. angry   **b.** sad   **c.** excited

2. Why do the children think the fish are biting?

   a. The fish are jumping out of the water.

   b. Many people are fishing.

   c. It is a sunny day.

UNIT 9 Being Afraid • **Lesson 2** *My Brother Is Afraid of Just About Everything*

▶ Synonyms

▸Read each sentence. Circle the words that make sense in each sentence. Write one of the synonyms on the lines.

(hard)	rush	hurry	(difficult)

_____

1. The homework was ____ hard or difficult ____.

(clever)	forest	(bright)	woods

_____

2. Nate had a ____ clever or bright ____ idea.

(students)	scary	frightening	(pupils)

_____

3. The ____ students or pupils ____ followed the teacher's directions.

VOCABULARY

UNIT 9 Being Afraid • **Lesson 2** *My Brother Is Afraid of Just About Everything*

▶ Sound Spelling Review

 Circle the words with the /ā/ sound. Draw a line under the words with the /ō/ sound.

(train)	sand	rose	not	those	(way)
(face)	cat	pond	wrote	(stay)	(wait)

Write a sentence using one of the circled words.

_____
— — — — — — Sentences will vary. — — — — — — —

Write a sentence using one of the underlined words.

— — — — — — Sentences will vary. — — — — — — —

Write two more words with the /n/ sound spelled *kn_*.

_____   _____

knees — — — — — — **Answers will vary.** — — — — —

Write two more words with the /ar/ sound spelled *ar*.

_____   _____

card — — — — — **Answers will vary.** — — — — — —

Sound Spelling Review • Challenge: Comprehension and Language Arts Skills

Name _____ Date _____

▶ End Rhyme

▶ **Write rhyming words to finish each poem.**

1. I want to sing   _____

When I hear the bells _____ ring _____.

2. She said to the bee,   _____

"Would you like to drink _____ tea _____
With Molly and me?"

3. The little black dog
Ran down to the park.

_____

He saw a green _____ frog _____

_____

And started to _____ bark _____.

WRITER'S CRAFT

▶ Context Clues

▶Read each sentence. Use the context clues to help you understand what the underlined word means. Write the word from the box that means the same as the underlined word.

work	answer	test	artist

1. The things we learned in school were on the final

   exam. _____test_____

2. I need a <u>reply</u> to my question. ___answer___

3. An <u>illustrator</u> painted the pictures in the book.

   ___artist___

4. The men will <u>labor</u> all day lifting heavy boxes.

   ___work___

Context Clues • Challenge: Comprehension and Language Arts Skills

Name _____ Date _____

▶Review

▶ **Read the advertisement for Joe's Playland.**
Find 6 verbs and write them on the lines.

Joe's Playland

Eat Pizza!   Watch Movies!
Play Games!   Sing Songs!   Drink Soda!

Come Today!

Verbs, in any order:

_____   _____   _____

Eat   **Watch**   **Play**

_____   _____   _____

_____   _____   _____

Sing   **Drink**   **Come**

▶ **What are some things that you like to do? Write the**
action words on the lines.

_____   _____   _____

_____   _____   _____

Verbs will vary.

GRAMMAR AND USAGE

UNIT 9 Being Afraid • **Lesson 4** *We're Going on a Bear Hunt*

▶Sound Spelling Review

 Read each sentence. Circle the misspelled word. Write the word correctly in a sentence of your own.

SPELLING

1. The dog will (beeg) at the table.

_____

sentence using "beg" _____

2. The lake is (depe).

_____

sentence using "deep" _____

3. We (clep) our hands to the music.

_____

sentence using "clap" _____

4. I've been to the fair a (fue) times.

_____

sentence using "few" _____

5. Jen went on a biking (tripp).

_____

sentence using "trip" _____

6. I looked (selly) on the tiny bike.

_____

sentence using "silly" _____

Sound Spelling Review • **Challenge: Comprehension and Language Arts Skills**

▶The Suffix -er

▶ Add *-er* to each word to make it mean "more."
Write the word on the line. Then write a sentence
using that *-er* word.

1. bright

brighter

Sentences will vary; check for meaning.

2. long

longer

Sentences will vary; check for meaning.

3. quiet

quieter

Sentences will vary; check for meaning.

4. soft

softer

Sentences will vary; check for meaning.

VOCABULARY

► # Review

▶ **Write sentences that end with the marks shown in the boxes.**

1. Sentences will vary.

2. _____

3. _____

4. _____

5. _____

6. _____

Review • Challenge: Comprehension
and Language Arts Skills

▶Comparing and Contrasting

▶Circle the pictures that are alike. Write a sentence telling how they are alike.

Sentence will vary. Possible answer:

Both pictures are trucks.

▶Circle the picture that is different. Write a sentence telling how it is different.

Sentence will vary. Possible answer:

The man is sawing wood.

COMPREHENSION

▶Sound Spelling Review

 Write each word from the box under the word that has the same vowel sound.

SPELLING

soon	cube	grew	tube
unit	music	huge	food

/o͞o/

moon

_____

soon

_____

grew

_____

tube

_____

food

/ū/

mule

_____

music

_____

unit

_____

cube

_____

huge

Accept answers in any order.

 Circle the words from the box that have the /kw/ sound spelled *qu_*. Write the *qu_* words on the lines.

(square)   spill   (quit)   curb   (quick)

any order:

_____   _____   _____

square   quit   quick

Sound Spelling Review • Challenge: Comprehension and Language Arts Skills

▶Review

▶Read the sentences. Circle the adjective in each sentence. Add *–er* to the adjective and write a sentence that compares two things. Add *–est* to the adjective and write a sentence that compares more than two things. The first one is done for you.

1. The chair is (high.)

    Add *–er*   **The stool is higher than the chair.**

    Add *–est*   **The table is the highest of all.**

2. An apple is (sweet.)

   "sweeter" should compare two things in a sentence.

   "sweetest" should compare more than two things in a sentence.

3. The cat is (big.)

   "bigger" should compare two things in a sentence.

   "biggest" should compare more than two things in a sentence.

GRAMMAR AND USAGE

▶Cause and Effect

▶**What caused each effect? Write a sentence for each.**

Accept any reasonable sentences.

1. The pie is steaming.

It just came out of the oven.

2. They are giving the dog a bath.

The dog played in mud.

3. Jill is covering her ears.

The thunder is loud.

4. The children are going outside.

It is time for recess.

Cause and Effect • Challenge: Comprehension and Language Arts Skills

▶Compound Words

▶Use the words in the box to make new compound words. You may use some words more than once.

mail	bed	walk	book	note
air	in	out	box	lock
room	side	case	pad	plane

_____ Possible compound words: _____

mailbox, bedroom, sidewalk, outside, inside, bookcase,

airplane, notepad, notebook, padlock, mailroom

▶Choose a compound word above and use it in a sentence.

_____

Sentences may vary; check for meaning.

VOCABULARY

▶ Sound Spelling Review

Write each word from the box under the word that has the same vowel sound.

out	try	own	apply
party	grow	story	down

Accept answers in any order.

/ow/

ouch

out

down

/ō/

slow

own

grow

/ē/ spelled _y

happy

party

story

/ī/ spelled _y

cry

try

apply

Sound Spelling Review • Challenge: Comprehension and Language Arts Skills

▶Review

▶Complete each sentence with a past tense verb.

Accept any reasonable past tense verbs.

1. Jack _____ to catch the bus.

2. The dog _____ onto the bed.

3. Fay _____ her lunch.

4. Dan _____ down the hill on his sled.

5. Mom _____ on the icy path.

6. The vase _____ to the floor.

7. The ball _____ the window.

GRAMMAR AND USAGE

VOCABULARY

▶Review

▸**Write a sentence using the word *neighbor*. Use context clues that might help a younger person figure out what the word *neighbor* means.**

1. _____ Sentence will vary; check for context clues. _____

▸**Write a pair of synonyms that describe the weather where you live today.**

2. ___ Synonyms will vary. ___   3. _____

▸**Complete the meaning for the word *older*.**

4. older   more _____ old _____

▸**Write four different words that can join the word *any* to form a compound word. Possible words:**

any _____ one _____   any _____ thing _____

any _____ where _____   any _____ way _____

Review • Challenge: Comprehension and Language Arts Skills

▶Rhythm

▶ **Read the poem. Clap the beat. Write a poem about school with the same beat.**

Twinkle, twinkle little star

How I wonder what you are

Up above the world so high

Like a diamond in the sky.

_____
- -
_____ everyday

- -
_____ play

- -
_____ need

- -
_____ read.

Check to see that students use the same rhythm as "Twinkle, Twinkle Little Star."

WRITER'S CRAFT

▶Sound Spelling Review

SPELLING

 Write a word that rhymes with each spelling word.

Rhyming words will vary.

1. law _____   **3.** sting _____

2. fawn _____   **4.** fling _____

Circle the words that have long-vowel sounds + *r*.

(stair)   (more)   fur   car   (roar)   (share)

▶Write a sentence using each of the circled words.

_____
Sentence using the word "stair".
_____

_____
Sentence using the word "more".
_____

_____
Sentence using the word "roar".
_____

_____
Sentence using the word "share".

▶Review

▶Circle the verb that agrees with the naming part of the sentence.

1. The children (work) / works outside in the garden.

2. Mike and Steve (prepare) / prepares the soil.

3. Susan plant / (plants) the seeds.

▶Write a sentence about something that you can do outside. Underline the naming part of your sentence. Circle the verb. Be sure that the verb agrees with the naming part.

_____

- -

Sentences will vary.

_____

GRAMMAR AND USAGE

▶Classifying and Categorizing

COMPREHENSION

Read the words in the box. Write each word below the category in which it belongs.

seeds	ball	hose	shovel
rain	net	mitt	helmet

Things for gardening

_____

seeds

_____

hose

_____

shovel

_____

rain

Things for sports

_____

ball

_____

net

_____

mitt

_____

helmet

▶Parts of a Group

▶Write four words that name a kind of fruit.

_____   _____

_ _ _ _ _ _ _ _ _ _ _ _   _ _ _ _ _ _ _ _ _ _ _ _

_____   _____

_____   _____

_ _ _ _ _ _ _ _ _ _ _ _   _ _ _ _ _ _ _ _ _ _ _ _

_____   _____

Possible answers: apple, banana, pear, grapes

▶Write four words that name a kind of vegetable.

_____   _____

_ _ _ _ _ _ _ _ _ _ _ _   _ _ _ _ _ _ _ _ _ _ _ _

_____   _____

_____   _____

_ _ _ _ _ _ _ _ _ _ _ _   _ _ _ _ _ _ _ _ _ _ _ _

_____   _____

Possible answers: carrots, celery, peas, spinach

▶Write two words that name a dairy product.

_____   _____

_ _ _ _ _ _ _ _ _ _ _ _   _ _ _ _ _ _ _ _ _ _ _ _

_____   _____

Possible answers: milk, cheese

VOCABULARY

► Sound Spelling Review

► **Complete each word by writing *oi* or *oy*.**

The birthday b_____oy_____ will be here soon.

Shhh! Don't sp_____oi_____l the surprise!

► **Complete each word with the /j/ sound by writing *dge* or *ge* or *gi_* in each blank.**

The _____ge_____ntle _____gi_____ant would not bu_____dge_____.

► **Complete each word with /s/ spelled *ce* or *ci*, /ch/ spelled *ch*, or /er/ spelled *er, ir, ur***

The _____ch_____ildren sat in a _____ci_____rcle to help bake.

A g_____ir_____l added the spi_____ce_____s.

Sound Spelling Review • Challenge: Comprehension
and Language Arts Skills

▶Classifying and Categorizing

Circle the word that does not fit into each category.

1. Things to eat

apple   carrot   (pan)   potato

2. Things that fly

airplane   bird   butterfly   (rock)

3. Things to wear

(fan)   shirt   hat   sock

4. Things to read

book   (lamp)   map   newspaper

5. Art supplies

(truck)   glue   crayon   paint

6. Farm Animals

cow   (tiger)   horse   pig

COMPREHENSION

►Parts of a Group

VOCABULARY

►Write a list of words that name people and a list of words that name animals.

People	Animals
Possible answers:	Possible answers:
People:	Animals:
boy, girl, baby, man, woman	cat, dog, rabbit, cow, horse

►Write a sentence about a person on your list.

_____

Sentences will vary.

►Write a sentence about an animal on your list.

_____

Sentences will vary.

▶ Sound Spelling Review

▶ **Circle the words with the /ar/ sound.**

(barn)   (farm)   balloon   (garden)

pencil   (cartons)   (marbles)   book

(started)   bird   (sharp)   (jar)

 Write the correct spelling word next to its meaning clue. Then, write a sentence using that word.

1. having an edge or point ____ sharp ____

_____

Sentence using the word "sharp."

2. a large farm building or shed ____ barn ____

_____

Sentence using the word "barn."

SPELLING

UNIT 10 Homes • **Lesson 4** *A House Is a House for Me*

▶Review

Write the correct contraction for each pair of words. Then, use the contraction in a sentence.

GRAMMAR USAGE AND MECHANICS

1. are not _____ aren't _____

Sentences will vary.

2. he will _____ he'll _____

3. I am _____ I'm _____

Review • Challenge: Comprehension and Language Arts Skills

▶ Exact Words

Draw a picture of yourself at a friend's house. Write sentences using exact words to describe what is happening in your picture.

WRITER'S CRAFT

Students should write sentences using exact nouns,

adjectives, and vivid verbs.

▶ Compound Words

Read the words. Write the second part of each word to make a compound word. Write a sentence using each compound word. Accept correct compound words.

1. rain _____ Possible answers: bow, drop, coat.

   _____

   Sentences will vary.

2. book _____ Possible answers: case, shelf, mark.

   _____

   Sentences will vary.

3. house _____ Possible answers: fly, plant, keeper.

   _____

   Sentences will vary.

Compound Words • Challenge: Comprehension and Language Arts Skills

Name _____ Date _____

▶Review

Write the correct possessive phrase and write the
possessive phrase using a pronoun for each picture.

Janet   books

bird   cage

_____

- -

Janet's books

bird's cage

_____

- -

her books

its cage

Kenny   camera

baby   bib

_____

- -

Kenny's camera

baby's bib

_____

- -

his camera

her bib

GRAMMAR AND USAGE

▶ Main Idea and Details

▶ **Circle the sentences that belong with the main idea.**

Main Idea: Playing Games
Details:

1. This afternoon, Sue's sister played tennis with her friend Jane.

2. Joe goes to soccer practice everyday after school.

3. Sally lost the button on her coat.

4. Sara hit a home run today at her softball game.

5. Bob did not pack his lunch.

6. Matt ran the last leg of the relay race.

7. Lisa was sick and couldn't go outside.

8. Angie and Lori play board games on rainy days.

Main Idea and Details • Challenge: Comprehension and Language Arts Skills

UNIT 10 Homes • **Lesson 6** *Make a Home*

▶Sound Spelling Review

▶Complete the words by writing *ph* or *f*.

_____f_____inds   al_____ph_____abet

tele_____ph_____one   _____f_____irst

▶Add the /k/ sound to each word by writing *c, k,* or *_ck.*

_____c_____arrying   lu_____ck_____

el_____k_____   _____c_____rawl

s_____k_____un_____k_____s   cra_____ck_____

SPELLING

WRITER'S CRAFT

▶ Sensory Details

Write describing words in each sentence.

_____

- - - - - - - - - -

1. A bird's nest is made of _____ twigs and string.

_____   _____

- - - - - - - - -   - - - - - - - - -

2. A rabbit's home is _____ and _____.

_____

- - - - - - - - -

3. Spiders spin webs with _____ threads.

_____ _____

- - - - - - - - - - - - - - - - - -

4. Fish live in the _____ _____ sea.

Answers will vary. Students should write appropriate adjectives for each animal home.

Sensory Details • Challenge: Comprehension and Language Arts Skills

▶Making Inferences

What might be happening? Write three sentences.

Answers will vary. Possible answers:

1. _____ The cat wants to jump off the bookcase. _____

2. _____ The girls are having a sleepover. _____

3. _____ The boy likes to play baseball. _____

▶ Parts of a Group

VOCABULARY

▶ **All of the words below name things in a kitchen.**
Write each word from the box where it fits the best.

fork	dishes	pans

1. pots   and   _____
   pans
   _____

2. spoon   and   _____
   fork
   _____

3. cups   and   _____
   dishes

▶ **Write more words that name things that can be found in a kitchen.**

_____   _____

_____   _____

_____   _____

Answers will vary; check for meaning.

▶Review

▶**Add quotation marks to the conversation.**

"What do you like to do at school?" asked Dora."Do you like math and science?"

"I am good at math,"said Bob."I can add and subtract."

"I like to read,"said Dora."Books tell exciting stories."

"Recess is always fun!"laughed Bob. "My friends and I like to play tag."

▶**Write your answer to Dora's question on the line. Use your exact words.**

What do you like to do at school?

_____

- -

" **Answers will vary.** "
_____

MECHANICS

UNIT 10 Homes • **Lesson 8** *Is This a House for Hermit Crab?*

▶ Sound Spelling Review

Read the paragraph. Underline the misspelled words. Write the words correctly on the lines.

The Pet Store

I was <u>walkng</u> <u>alog</u> the sidewalk when I saw a pet store. Something was <u>peerng</u> out the window at me. It <u>riggled</u> and wagged its tail. It was a puppy <u>playng</u>! I wanted to play with the pup, but I looked at the watch on my <u>rist</u> and saw that it was time to go home.

walking	peering
along	wriggled
playing	wrist

Sound Spelling Review • Challenge: Comprehension and Language Arts Skills

SPELLING

▶A Friendly Letter

Write a friendly letter telling about a friend's home you have visited.

Letters will vary.
Students should have all parts of
the letter correctly placed.

▶ # Reality and Fantasy

Write two sentences about something real in the picture. Then write two sentences about something make believe.

COMPREHENSION

Real

Sentences will vary.

_____

- -

The man pays for the gas.

_____

- -

The girl sits on the curb.

_____

Make-believe

_____

- -

A tiger washes the windows.

_____

- -

A kangaroo takes the money.

UNIT 10 Homes • **Lesson 9** *The Three Little Pigs*

▶Parts of a Group

▶Write words that describe the way you are feeling today.

_____   _____

_ _ _ _ _ _ _ _ _ _   _ _ _ _ _ _ _ _ _ _
Answers will vary.
_____   _____

_ _ _ _ _ _ _ _ _ _   _ _ _ _ _ _ _ _ _ _

_____   _____

▶Draw a picture that shows how you are feeling today.

▶Write a sentence using one of your feeling words above.

_____

_ _
Sentences will vary.
_____

VOCABULARY

MECHANICS

▶Review

Read the invitation. Look for mistakes in capitalization. Rewrite the invitation and correct all the mistakes.

What?   a party for pedro

When?   sunday, april 23

Where?   74 bennett street

red hill, iowa

_____

What?   **A party for Pedro**

_____

When?   **Sunday, April 23**

_____

Where?   **74 Bennett Street**

_____

Red Hill, Iowa

Review • Challenge: Comprehension and Language Arts Skills

▶Audience and Purpose

Read the name of the audience. Write a purpose to tell why you would write a letter to each one.

WRITER'S CRAFT

1. Your neighbor

_____

2. Your principal

_____

3. A shop owner

_____

4. A television station

_____

5. Your aunt or uncle

_____

6. Your local newspaper _____

Answers will vary.

The purpose should be appropriate for the audience.

▶ Sound Spelling Review

Write the correct spelling word next to its meaning clue. Then, write a sentence using that word.

coin	strong	third

_____

- - - - - - - - -

1. a small piece of metal used as money _____ *coin*

_____

- -

Sentence with the word "coin."

_____

_____

- - - - - - - - -

2. having great muscle power _____ *strong*

_____

- -

Sentence with the word "strong."

_____

_____

- - - - - - - - -

3. between second and fourth _____ *third*

_____

- -

Sentence with the word "third."

_____

Sound Spelling Review • **Challenge: Comprehension and Language Arts Skills**